Ecology

Donna Latham

Raintree

Chicago, Illinois

©2009 Raintree
an imprint of Capstone Global Library, LLC
Chicago, Illinois

Edited by Adam Miller, Andrew Farrow, and
Adrian Vigliano
Designed by Philippa Jenkins and Ken Vail
Original illustrations © Capstone Global Library
Limited 2009
Illustrated by Gary Joynes p8, 34, 35; Ian Escott p11, 13;
Maurizio De Angelis p15, 17
Picture research by Ruth Blair
Originated by Raintree
Printed and bound in China by South China Printing
Company Ltd.

13 12 11 10 09
10 9 8 7 6 5 4 3 2 1

Library of Congress Cataloging-in-Publication Data
Latham, Donna.
Ecology / Donna Latham.
p. cm. -- (Sci-hi. Life science)
Includes bibliographical references and index.
ISBN 978-1-4109-3328-7 (hc) -- ISBN 978-1-4109-
3336-2 (pb) 1. Ecology--Juvenile literature. I. Title.
QH541.14.L364 2009
577--dc22
2009003465

Acknowledgments
The publishers would like to thank the following for
permission to reproduce copyright material:
iStockphoto/Rick Carroll p. **iii** (contents top);
iStockphoto/Frank Leung p. **iii** (contents bottom);
Alamy/WorldFoto p. **4**; FLPA/Mitsuaki Iwago/Minden
Pictures p. **5**; FLPA/ p. **7**; SCIENCE PHOTO LIBRARY/
JOHN DURHAM p. **9**; Alamy/blickwinkel p. **10**; NHPA/
Martin Harvey p. **12**; NHPA/Martin Harvey p. **14**;
Alamy/Noella Ballenger p. **17**; Getty Images/Alfred
Eisenstaedt; Time Life Pictures p. **18**; iStockphoto/
Frank Leung p. **19**; SCIENCE PHOTO LIBRARY/JOHN
MITCHELL p. **20**; Photos by Clay DeGayner p. **21**;
iStockphoto/Tammy Peluso p. **22**; iStockphoto/ p. **23**;
naturepl.com/Kim Taylor p. **25**; naturepl.com/Simon
King p. **26**; iStockphoto/ p. **27**; iStockphoto/Roger
Whiteway p. **28**; NHPA/Stephen Dalton p. **29**; FLPA/S &
D & K Maslowski p. **30**; iStockphoto/Rick Carroll p. **31**;
iStockphoto/ Govert Nieuwland p. **32**; Art Directors
and Trip/Helene Rogers p. **33**; Reuters/Punit Paranjpe
p. **36**; iStockphoto/Pauline Mills p. **37**; FLPA/Tony
Hamblin p. **38**; Shutterstock/Geoff Delderfield p. **39**;
SCIENCE PHOTO LIBRARY/NASA p. **40**; Shutterstock
background images and design features.

Cover photo of an anemonefish in anemone used with
permission of Photolibrary/Carol Buchanan **main**.
Cover image of a dung beetle/scarab beetle used with
permission of Alamy/© Arco Images GmbH **inset**.

The publishers would like to thank literacy consultant
Nancy Harris and content consultant Michael Bright
for their assistance in the preparation of this book.

Contents

What almost killed off the bald eagle?

Go to page 19 to find out!

What is this fox doing in the city?

Turn to page 31 to find out!

Some words are shown in bold, **like this**. These words are explained in the glossary. You will find important information and definitions underlined, <u>like this</u>.

INTERACTION WITH THE ENVIRONMENT

Lounging on a tree limb, a leopard eyes you suspiciously. Cubs huddle in high grasses below her. A herd of zebra thunders across vast grasslands. Above you, on a soaring plateau, a waterfall rushes.

It's taken you a long time to get here, traveling by 4 x 4 through the rainy season. But it's worth the journey! Welcome to Nyika National Park. Spread across about 3,200 square kilometers (1,250 square miles) in Malawi, Africa, it's one of the most spectacular **ecosystems** on Earth.

An ecosystem is a group of living and nonliving things. They all live in the same **environment**, or natural surroundings. These animals, plants, and **microorganisms** (tiny organisms) are interdependent. They can't live without one another. They constantly interact. They relate with their environment, too. Living and nonliving things both affect and are affected by their surroundings.

Nyika National Park is home to central Africa's greatest number of leopards.

In Nyika National Park, scattered shrubs and trees rise over grasses. The endangered zebra is one inhabitant of the national park. Zebras are grazing members of the horse family. How do they depend on their environment? Zebras require plenty of space to roam. They need a good water source. That's why herds never wander more than 32 kilometers (20 miles) from watering holes.

Zebras also depend on their herds. When predators such as leopards and cheetahs attack one zebra, the herd responds. The herd bunches together and confronts the enemy. They stare down the predator until it runs away.

Zebras need plenty of space to graze for food.

Did You Know?

No two people have identical fingerprints, and no two zebras have the exact same pattern of stripes. Scientists believe the unique patterns help zebras identify one another in large herds.

Ecosystems—Staying Alive

Ecosystems are dynamic. They burst with energy. Their members perform jobs to keep their natural surroundings alive and balanced. **A healthy ecosystem includes the components, or parts, below. Working together, the parts form a system.**

Components of a balanced ecosystem

✓ Sun's energy

✓ defined boundaries, such as a pond or a meadow

✓ plants and animals

✓ dead organisms, including rotting plants and decaying animals

✓ nonliving things, including rocks and water

Common confusion

Some people confuse the terms biome and **ecosystem**. A biome is a large geographical area where certain vegetation grows. It features a certain climate and soil. Specific plants and animals inhabit it. For example, the desert is a biome. In contrast, an ecosystem has smaller boundaries. A 15-meter (50-foot) saguaro cactus in New Mexico's Sonora Desert forms the center of an ecosystem.

A saguaro cactus

A rocky area defines the ecosystem's boundaries. Scorching Sun, a nonliving thing, shines overhead. Yet, a hole in a cool cactus provides a safe place for an elf owl's nest. The owl enjoys a birds-eye view of tasty scorpions below. When the saguaro's flowers bloom, bats, insects, and birds sip sweet nectar. They flit from blossom to blossom and spread pollen. That helps fruit grow. Later, fruit and seeds fall to the ground. Hungry coyotes and javelinas gobble them. When these animals spread seeds, more cacti grow.

Saguaro can live for 150 years! When this one dies, its pulpy flesh will plop to the desert floor. With the help of insects and bacteria, it rots. Decomposed, it becomes part of the desert's gritty soil.

ecosystem

Did you know?

Terrestrial ecosystems are located on land. Aquatic ecosystems are found in water.

The saguaro cactus can become a home to many animals, including these elf owls.

SUNLIGHT AND PHOTOSYNTHESIS

Whether in a desert or a rain forest, ecosystems depend on the Sun. Sunlight produces all of Earth's energy. The Sun's energy is called solar energy.

<u>In ecosystems, plants make their own food. They convert solar energy to chemical energy through **photosynthesis.**</u> How? Plants use sunlight, water (H_2O) from soil, and carbon dioxide gas (CO_2) from air. Read the panel and study the diagram to discover how plants combine the three ingredients.

event

From Sunlight to Energy

Through roots, plants suck water from the ground. They take in carbon dioxide through stomata. **Stomata** are microscopic **pores** (tiny openings) on the underside of leaves. They open and shut like mouths. Stomata allow water and gases to pass in and out of the plant.

Did you know leaves are a plant's food factories? Inside leaf **cells** (the smallest parts of organisms) are **chloroplasts.** Chloroplasts are tiny solar panels, built to capture sunlight. Inside them is **chlorophyll,** a green **pigment** (color).

Chloroplasts perform photosynthesis. They turn the three ingredients into **carbohydrates,** such as glucose. That's a simple sugar. Carbohydrates feed the plant. But that's not all. As the first link in the **food chain,** they also fuel animals. People, too. (You'll learn more about the food chain on page 10!)

Plants **respire,** or use energy from food, as part of photosynthesis. <u>When plants respire they use oxygen to break down sugar.</u> They release carbon dioxide.

Chloroplasts in leaf cells perform photosynthesis.

Solar energy

Oxygen, O_2

Chloroplasts

Carbon Dioxide, CO_2

Water, H_2O

Stomata

Food Chains, Food Webs, and Energy Pyramids

A **community** is formed of organisms that live and interact in one natural area. <u>Food chains show what members of a community eat.</u>

Producers and consumers

Solar energy passes from one organism to another. You've learned plants make their own food through **photosynthesis**. They also supply food for animals. Plants are **producers**, the first link in the chain. **Consumers** come next. Consumers are animals, and they eat producers. For example, chipmunks eat berries.

Herbivores eat only plant food, including grass and stems. They eat seeds, flowers, fruit, and bark. Grasshoppers, goats, and gorillas are herbivores. So are bees, deer, and hippos.

Omnivores feed on plants and animals. For example, grizzly bears feast on grasses and berries. But they also eat wasps, fish, and goats. Chickens, raccoons, and foxes are omnivores. So are many people.

When herbivores and omnivores eat, the Sun's energy moves up the chain. **Carnivores** reign at the top. These meat-eating predators prey on other animals. Cougars, lions, and sharks are carnivores.

Hippos are nocturnal grazers. These herbivores wander at night to find plant food.

Decomposers

Food chains depend on **decomposers**. Decomposers do an ecosystem's dirty work. They eat wastes and devour dead plants and animals. **Fungi**, (organisms that make spores and don't use photosynthesis, such as molds and mushrooms) bacteria, and insects are decomposers. They break down the dead. Through soil, decomposers send nutrients back into the ecosystem. Plants absorb nutrients. Stored energy in producers transfers through the chain.

wild dog
(carnivore)

Missing from the chain

One part of a food chain depends on another. Imagine an ecosystem with only producers and consumers. Over time, plants will deplete minerals from the soil. Without minerals, plants die. A chain reaction then launches. Herbivores have nothing to eat. Without plants and herbivores to feed on, omnivores starve. Soon, even mighty carnivores perish. No longer balanced, the ecosystem dies.

baboon
(omnivore)

A savanna food chain

dung beetle
(decomposer)

grasshopper
(herbivore)

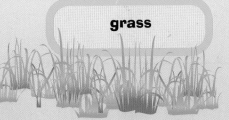

grass

Food webs

A food chain illustrates one path of energy. For example, the chain on page 11 shows a simple path:

Grass → Grasshopper → Baboon → Wild Dog

But ecosystems aren't simple. They are made up of a variety of plants and animals. Most animals feast on several foods. So they might be part of different chains.

In a single ecosystem, different chains share food sources. For example, the grasshopper eats grass. Yet, antelopes and wildebeests inhabit the same ecosystem. They feed on grass too. In the illustration on page 11 you notice a wild dog preys on the baboon. Leopards and cheetahs, neighbors in the ecosystem, enjoy the same dinner.

These feeding relationships are more complicated. **Food webs illustrate the way food chains connect.** Like food chains, their energy flow begins with plants. Study the food web on the right to trace the different paths of energy that flow through it.

In a savanna food web, a carcass provides food for several different animals.

A savanna food web

THE LION is the top carnivore.

THE WILD DOG eats the wildebeest, antelope and the baboon.

WILDEBEEST

ANTELOPE

THE BABOON eats the grasshopper.

GRASSHOPPER

GRASS is the food source for the wildebeest, antelope, grasshopper, and baboon.

DUNG BEETLES are decomposers that break down dead organisms.

DEAD ORGANISM

Energy pyramids

Biomass is renewable organic (living) material. It can be grown, used, and then grown again. Photosynthesis produces and increases plant biomass. In turn, when herbivores consume plants, their own biomass increases.

Biomass contains stored energy from the Sun. **An energy pyramid illustrates energy transfer in feeding patterns.** Each level shows how energy flows when one organism eats another. Study the pyramid on page 15. Notice that levels get smaller as they move up? That's because energy flow decreases as it passes along. Only about 10 percent flows to the next level.

The bottom level is largest. It contains plant biomass from producers. You know plants use the Sun's energy to grow. They stash extra energy. That's for the herbivores at the second level. When herbivores like giraffes and antelopes gobble plants, they consume the Sun's energy. Some gets stored in their bodies as fat and meat. Most is used right away for grazing, dodging predators, and staying alive. At the top of this pyramid rests a lone lion. With less energy to sustain them, top carnivores are fewer in number.

In the tropical savanna, a fierce lion preys on a plant-eating antelope.

Design an energy pyramid

Choose an ecosystem, such as a pond, a bog (area with wet, muddy ground), or a prairie. Research the types of producers and consumers that live there. Then design an energy pyramid that shows how specific producers and consumers pass energy. Look at the energy pyramid below as an example.

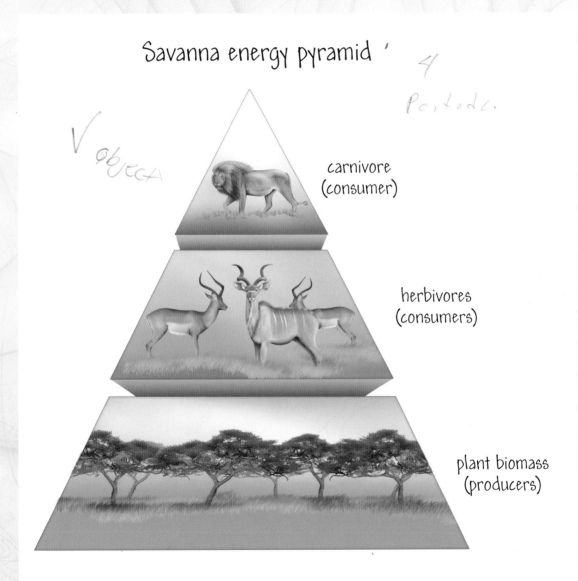

Savanna energy pyramid

carnivore
(consumer)

herbivores
(consumers)

plant biomass
(producers)

BIOMAGNIFICATION

What happens when a dangerous substance enters the food chain? It increases at each level. This process is biomagnification.

Spraying pesticides

In 1955, pesky insects invaded peach orchards in California. Valuable crops suffered. Crop dusters took to the skies. The small planes contained spraying systems in their wings. The dusters dipped over trees. They sprayed **pesticide**, a chemical that kills insects.

This is how biomagnification begins.

Pesticides move up the chain

Eventually, rainstorms sweep over the sprayed orchards. The water runs off and carries pesticide with it. It drains into a river, which flows into the Pacific Ocean. The pesticide contaminates, or pollutes, the ocean. Green algae in the water take in the pesticide. Algae are a group of simple plants that don't produce flowers.

When a small fish eats the algae, pesticide enters its body. The pesticide grows stronger or more concentrated. It adds to the pesticide levels the fish already took in. Soon, a seagull gulps down the fish. A higher concentration of pesticide enters the gull. Pesticide moves up the food chain.

On a rocky ledge over the ocean, a peregrine falcon swoops down. In midair, it captures the seagull in sharp talons. It devours the prey. Now, highly concentrated pesticide moves to the top of the chain.

Pesticide doesn't kill the falcon. However, it harms calcium in its body. The falcon needs calcium for healthy eggs. When it lays eggs, they are fragile. They crack under the falcon's weight.

BIOMAGNIFICATION

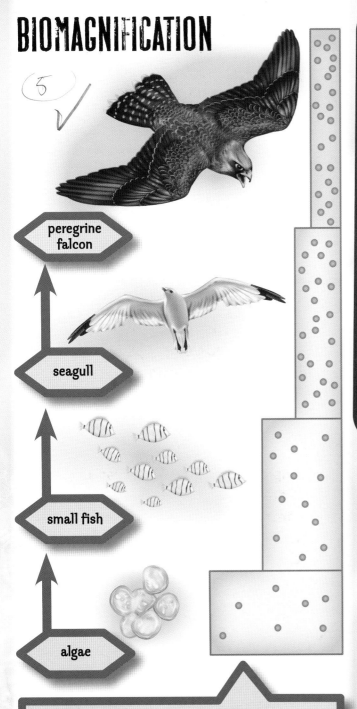

peregrine falcon

seagull

small fish

algae

A harmful substance can be dangerous to an animal if the animal comes into contact with it. But the same substance can be much more dangerous if that same animal eats another animal which has been exposed to the substance. This happens because of the way animals store substances in their fat.

Did you know?

The word *peregrine* comes from the Latin word *peregrinus*, which means "wanderer." These birds of prey wander every continent but Antarctica.

Other dangers

These other dangerous substances can enter food chains, as well.

◎ Dioxins (dangerous poisons produced as waste when things such as paper are made)

◎ Mercury (a very poisonous metal that is used in batteries and **electronics**)

◎ Radioactive waste (waste that is contaminated with radiation from nuclear reactions).

Rachel Carson
Ahead of Her Time

Rachel Carson was a renowned writer and **ecologist**. Born in 1907 in rural Springdale, Pennsylvania, she loved nature from an early age. She made the natural world her life's work.

Carson attended the Woods Hole Marine Biology Lab in Cape Cod, Massachusetts. Later, she earned a Master's degree in zoology (scientific study of animals). A talented writer, Carson penned radio scripts about natural history. She published poetic books about oceans. She expressed that people were part of nature and held power to change it. And not always for the better.

Silent Spring

Carson grew alarmed at the increased use of pesticides, especially the chemical DDT. She studied research about DDT and noted its effect on bald eagle eggs. They became thin-shelled and fragile. Carson warned that when pesticides pass through ecosystems, they affect all its members. In 1962, she published the book *Silent Spring*. She cautioned people that their actions created trouble for other living things.

Carson's research impacted scientific thought. Her writings launched the environmental movement. This is now made up of people and groups around the world who work to protect the environment. Rachel Carson affected the environment itself. Thanks to her efforts, in 1972 the United States government banned the use of DDT. In 1984, the United Kingdom banned DDT. Today, however, the pesticide is still used in some areas of the world.

Did you know?

In 1782, 75,000 bald eagles soared in the United States. By the 1960s, only 900 remained. In 2007, the population had rebounded to 9,789. Scientists believe this increase is directly related to the banning of DDT. Now the majestic eagles have flown off of the endangered species list.

Female bald eagles only lay about two to three eggs in a year. Because of this, the species almost went extinct due to the egg-weakening effects of DDT in the food chain.

person

Alien Invaders!

Wanted for trespassing—Burmese pythons. One of Earth's largest snakes, these gigantic constrictors weigh 115 kg (250 pounds). They stretch to 6 meters (20 feet). About ten years ago, the huge reptiles infiltrated the Florida Everglades. An invasive species, the python created trouble in the ecosystem.

What's an invasive species?

<u>An invasive species is not naturally found in a certain habitat. By entering a new ecosystem, aliens harm plants, animals, and people.</u> Burmese pythons' typical home is Asia. They live in Burma, China, Thailand, and Vietnam. Excellent swimmers, they thrive near water. They feast on birds, mammals, lizards, and amphibians.

The snakes prove highly adaptable. For ten years, they've made themselves at home in the Everglades. There, pythons encounter new foods. They gulp down Key Largo wood rats, which are endangered animals. They devour rare round-tailed muskrats. Pythons even battle alligators. (So far, there's no clear victor.)

Because there are so many of them in the wild, pythons are now considered to be the main predator in the Everglades.

Other animals in the Everglades, such as this endangered Key Largo woodrat, could be easily wiped out if the python problem continues.

Biologists grow concerned by threats to protected animals. They worry pythons might harm humans. What's more, biologists know people deliberately release pythons into the Everglades. When these exotic pets become too large for people to keep at home, they let them go in the wild.

Eyes and Ears Team

Now, the problem is spreading. In 2007, researchers noticed the superb swimmers invaded a new area. The pythons swam to the Florida Keys, about ten kilometers (six miles) from the Everglades.

Conservationists are working to halt the new invasion. They targeted workers, including postal drivers, safety officers, and gardening crews, and asked for help. Now, these workers are part of the special Eyes and Ears Team trained to spot the invaders. When they see a python, they call a hotline at the sheriff's office and wait near the snake. Meanwhile, the sheriff's office sends a handler to the spot to safely capture and remove the invader. So far, it's working. But conservationists worry invaders could swim to a new location.

Symbiosis

You've learned ecosystems burst with energy. Inhabitants interact and interconnect, especially through feeding patterns. Symbiosis is another way organisms connect. <u>Symbiosis occurs when two different species form relationships. Sometimes these relationships create mutual benefits.</u>

Mutualism

<u>Mutualism is a form of symbiosis. In this kind of relationship both species gain something.</u> The clown fish and the sea anemone share this kind of relationship. Both make their homes in saltwater coral reefs. Their partnership keeps both nourished and safe from enemies.

The anemone looks like an underwater flower. A member of the coral family, it's actually an animal. The anemone stings and paralyzes (stuns) prey with poisonous tentacles (a kind of flexible limb). Then, tentacles stuff motionless prey into an eager mouth.

A slimy surface shields the clown fish from toxic tentacles.

A clown fish lives fearlessly between the anemone's toxic tentacles. How? A slippery layer of mucus (a kind of slime made by the fish's body) coats the orange-and-white fish's body.

Mucus protects the clown fish from stings. The lively fish darts in and around the anemone. Its bright color and movements attract other fish, which the anemone stings and devours.

Clown fish seem frisky. They are actually **aggressive**. If another fish tries to prey on the anemone, the clown fish chases it. The clown fish not only receives a safe home in exchange for luring dinner to the anemone. It also gets the leftovers!

Did you know?

Clown fish are also called anemone fish. Clown fish usually live with mates. There's enough room for two in an anemone.

OTHER SYMBIOTIC RELATIONSHIPS

Research these odd partners to learn more about symbiosis:
◎ Dung beetles and skunk cabbage
◎ Egyptian plover and crocodile
◎ Oxpecker and impala

As part of a symbiotic relationship, impalas allow oxpecker birds to search their bodies for food. Oxpeckers will eat ticks and other parasites right off the impala's body. The oxpeckers get food and the impala has fewer pests!

Parasitism

Parasitism is a form of symbiosis. In a parasitic relationship, only one species benefits. The other suffers. It becomes weak, injured, or ill.

Parasitic relationships involve a parasite, a plant or animal that lives off a host. Imagine you take a dog for a walk in a wooded ecosystem. A flea, so tiny you don't see it, leaps off a shrub. The insect hops onto your dog. First, it sucks blood from the unwilling host. Then, the pesky parasite hitches a ride on the dog as you return home. Within weeks, the flea's offspring latch onto the poor pooch, too. Fortunately, you notice the pup's persistent itching. You visit the vet before fleas cause anemia, a condition that causes too few red blood cells to be produced.

Leeches and flukes

- Along with fleas, ticks and leeches cling to the outside of hosts. Leeches float in marshes and ponds. To feed, leeches latch onto fish, turtles, frogs, and people. With three sets of jaws, leeches gorge on blood and tissue.

- Other parasites, such as flukes and tapeworms, live inside hosts' organs. Flukes thrive in rain forest, forest, and grassland ecosystems. When they enter mammal hosts, flukes settle in the liver. They destroy tissue. Flukes cause liver rot, a disease that wipes out grazing sheep and cows.

Did you know?

Fleas duck their heads and tighten their bodies before hopping. They propel themselves with brawny hind legs. These wingless wonders can leap far—about 20 centimeters (8 inches) high and 38 centimeters (15 inches) long. That's nearly 200 times their own height! That's like an adult person jumping 37 meters (120 feet)!

Parasites, like this tick which is latched onto a larger animal's head, are typically smaller than their hosts.

Filling a Niche

You've learned ecosystems must remain balanced to survive. Each species in a community plays a certain role that contributes to the system to keep it balanced. This role is a **niche**. In an ecosystem, every species fills a niche.

Niches involve where species live, their feeding relationships, and their **foraging** habits (their searches to find food). Niches also include special activities that species engage in. Visit the Kalahari Desert in Botswana. Observe in action the busy meerkat. Through building and food-finding habits, the meerkat fills its niche.

A clan of meerkats usually numbers about 20. However some clans have been known to have 50 or more members!

Meerkat niche stats

Description:
Small, ground-dwelling member of the mongoose family

Where it lives:
In burrows in the Kalahari Desert, Africa

What it eats:
Carnivorous predator that eats eggs, spiders, lizards, and scorpions

Habits:
Builds **burrows** to escape heat and predators

Tunneling through soil, meerkats prevent soil erosion. Precious rainwater collects in burrows.

The Kalahari Desert

The Kalahari is a hostile environment. Rainfall is scarce, only 50 mm (2 inches) a year. Temperatures soar to 45 °C (113 °F). Large predators, lions, leopards, and cheetahs, reign at the top of the food chain. Cobras, raptors, and hyenas prey on reptiles, birds, rodents, and insects.

"Little earth men"

Meerkats face predators from sky and land. Hawks, eagles, and jackals are enemies. Sand provides a safer, cooler place to live. The German word for meerkats means "little earth men." These digging mammals create burrows, underground tunnels, in sandy soil.

Meerkats shovel through the soil with long claws. This helps seeds spread. Like mini farmers, meerkats loosen the ground. They allow air to reach plant roots.

Meerkats aren't fussy. They eat eggs, insects, spiders, and lizards. Just about anything on the Kalahari's menu. Meerkats must carefully unearth and catch their favorite treat, stinging scorpions. They also enjoy juicy insects that gnaw through roots. They eat locusts, ants, and termites that damage plants.

COMPETITION

A pair of 136 kilogram (300 pound) red stags lock antlers. They roar and push. The stags fight over potential mates. An enormous old oak tree stretches high. It snatches sunlight away from a seedling, which withers and dies. A gray squirrel stashes nuts under a log. It conceals others inside a shrub and buries more at the base of a stump. With more than one food-hiding place, the squirrel prevents a chipmunk from stealing all of its food.

Species compete

In ecosystems, species compete for food, water, sunlight, and mates. Hawks, eagles, and jackals, for example, compete for meerkats in the Kalahari. **Competition is the struggle for survival between species for the same limited resources.** Competition occurs within species, as it does with the stags battling for mates. Competition over food takes place between different species, like the squirrel and chipmunk.

Red deer stags battle for a mate.

Competition changes ecosystems

Competition can cause changes in ecosystems. In 2007, scientists conducted a study in Antarctica. They noted fur seals and macaroni penguins competed for the same food, krill. Both species dove deep in the waters to hunt for the shrimp-like creature. Gradually, the seal population grew. Seals consumed greater amounts of krill. Competition increased, and the seals gained the upper hand (or flipper)! With less to eat, the penguin population decreased.

Squirrels store seeds and nuts for the winter by hiding them in many small hiding places. Some scientists think that natural competition may sometimes cause squirrels to steal the stored food of other squirrels!

Roaming Raccoons

As people doze, **nocturnal** looters prowl the neighborhood. Trashcans rattle. Lids fall to the pavement. Masked raiders topple a can. They swarm inside to steal the contents. A band of burglars? Nope, it's a gaze, or group of raccoons.

One evening, a well-meaning person sets out a plate of scraps for the raccoons. The next night, the raccoons come back to the new food source with a few pals. Those buddies in turn share the wealth. They alert others in the gaze. Soon, 24 ravenous raccoons swarm the neighborhood every night. They rip open window screens with razor-sharp claws. They climb into attics and squeeze under porches to snooze during the days.

In the wild, raccoons thrive in wooded areas near water. Raccoons are skilled swimmers and spectacular climbers. They scramble up tall trees and descend headfirst as they search for shelter and food.

Omnivorous raccoons aren't picky eaters. They hunt small rodents, frogs, and crayfish. They steal duck and turtle eggs from nests, claw worms from the ground, and eat berries and nuts.

When a natural habitat shrinks or vanishes, raccoons scavenge for food in urban areas.

Changed Ecosystems

Yet, human activity changes natural ecosystems. People clear wooded areas to build homes and businesses. Then, raccoons and other wildlife invade urban areas.

Clever and resourceful, raccoons adapt quickly to a new environment.

They scavenge for food at night and discover easy pickings in dumpsters and trash cans. Raccoons feast on items unheard of in the wild. They devour pepperoni pizza, nachos, and cherry pie. What hungry prowler wouldn't hang around?

URBAN FOXES

It's not just raccoons that roam into urban areas when habitats change. In many European cities, people report city foxes trotting through pedestrian crossings and rummaging through trash.

In Africa, elephants and rhinos charge through farms and urban areas.

As suburbs grow in the Midwest, black bears wander across highways and into backyards. Birdfeeders and garbage provide easy pickings.

Red foxes have been able to adapt to changing natural habitats. Cities in several continents around the world are seeing red fox populations rise. They survive by eating everything from rats to garbage!

ECOLOGICAL SUCCESSION

Ecosystems are dynamic. They change constantly. As older organisms die, younger ones replace them. Some species die off completely. New species take hold in their place. **Ecological succession is the series of changes in communities that occurs over time.**

Changes in communities

You may have seen news stories about wildfires that wipe out forests. Or hurricanes that clobber coastal regions. Some changes in ecosystems occur because of these natural disasters. Human interference causes other changes. People slash and burn rain forests to clear land for building. Disastrous oil spills smother coral reefs. Other human-made changes such as overfishing (taking too many fish from a body of water) change ecosystems, too.

A violent act of nature

Visit southern Europe to witness a violent act of nature. Sicily's Mt. Etna rumbles. The volcano, over 3,048 meters (10,000 feet) high, erupts often. It spews fountains of molten rock. It blasts ash and toxic gases. Tongues of lava flow down the mountain. They scorch pine trees that grow nowhere else on the continent of Europe.

Mt. Etna is one of the world's most active volcanoes. It lies on African and Eurasian plates.

For weeks, tremendous amounts of volcanic ash shower the ecosystem. Ash smothers plants, which can't capture Sicily's sunlight. Olive crops shrivel. Lingering fires torch beech trees. And what about those pine trees that only grow on the mountain? Over 620 acres (250 hectares) burn away.

Nature's disturbance destroyed an ecosystem. Through the wonders of ecological succession, a new one takes its place. Turn the page to learn about its phases.

Did you know?

The ancient Greeks believed the one-eyed creature Cyclops lived in a cave at the base of Mt. Etna. In old tales, Cyclops was a powerful giant with a single eye in the middle of its forehead.

This woodcut of Mt. Etna erupting was made in the year 1669!

A Prospect of MOUNT ÆTNA, with its Irruption in 1669.
A Top of Ætna. B Irruption. C Two Hills made by the Irruption. D Fiery Currents. E The Arch of Marcellus. F City of Catania.
1 Montpileri. 2 La Guardia. 3 La Annunciata. 4 La Potielli. 5 Malpaſso. 6 Campo Rotundo. 7 St Pietro. 8 St Antonino. 9 Mosterbianco.
10 Falicchi. 11 Placchi. These Towns were quite Consumed, no Footsteps of them remaining. 12 St Giovanni de Galermo. 13 Mascalucia
hardly ruin'd by the Fiery Inundation. a. Nicolosi, wholly ruin'd by the Earthquake. b. Padara. c. Tre Castagne, ruin'd in part.

Stages of succession

After Mt. Etna's eruption, an ecosystem vanished. Where beech and pine trees once towered, rock, lava, and volcanic ash appear. The gray area appears barren. It falls quiet, without chattering birds and buzzing insects. In stages, vegetation spreads. Over time, the area transforms, like the stages of succession illustrated here.

STAGE ❶ Pioneers

You've probably read about brave pioneers. These adventurers ventured into unfamiliar territories. When they explored and settled new areas, they launched growth. Plant pioneers initiate growth, too. Pioneers are the first plant species to return to a disrupted area. First, **lichens** (simple plants formed from algae and fungus) and mosses cover the ground. Short tufts of grass spring up. Birds, insects, and worms return. Worms plow beneath soil, which becomes more fertile. Birds pluck worms from grasses and disperse seeds.

STAGE ❷
Herbaceous plants

Pioneers die. Decaying remains add nutrients to the soil. Now, ferns, weeds, and shrubs appear. Low to the ground, they grow in clumps. With more food available, small mammals and more birds settle in the area. Roaming, the mammals scatter seeds through their feces.

STAGE ❸ Small trees

With richer soil available, small trees, such as pines, take root. They compete for sunlight—and win. Their growth blocks sunlight from shrubs. The shrubs wither. Their decay fills the soil with more nutrients. Larger birds, including owls and hawks, move in. Foxes, weasels, and wildcats find plenty of prey among dormouse, mouse, and rabbit populations.

STAGE ❹
Climax

The climax stage is final. Now, birches, beeches, and oaks stand tall. In competition for Sun, they climbed high above small trees. It's taken 350 years. Yet, in its final stage, the recovered ecosystem is healthy and balanced.

Extinction: Gone Forever

Through ecological succession in a particular area, species come and go. Acts of nature, such as volcanoes and tsunamis (huge sea waves), kill them. Sometimes species vanish through human interference.

As they do in other places in the world, deer, wolves, and wild boars once roamed forests around Mt. Etna. As human populations increased, a greater need for homes developed. People cleared away trees to create space and building materials. Without homes and food, deer, wolves, and boars fled the ecosystem. Fortunately, they migrated to other areas, where they thrived.

What happens when a habitat is completely destroyed? Some species become extinct. **When a species is extinct, it no longer exists.** It's gone forever. Here are some examples of extinction's causes.

Disasters such as the Indian Ocean Tsunami of 2004 cause massive destruction. The most lethal geological event in history, the tsunami killed 220,000 people. Enormous waves swept away the eggs of endangered sea turtles, drawing them closer to extinction.

WHAT CAUSES EXTINCTION?

✓ **Climate change.** Higher temperatures cause Arctic ice to thin. Without ice to perch on, polar bears can't hunt for seals. The polar bear population has shrunk. In addition, seals and walruses, which share the ecosystem, are at risk.

✓ **Excessive hunting and trapping.** Some people kill great numbers of animals for meat, fur, shells, or skin. Have you heard of the dodo bird? The dodo once lived on the island of Mauritius in the Indian Ocean. When European explorers visited the island in the late 1500s, they over-hunted the turkey-sized bird and caused its extinction. In modern times, Asia's snow leopard has been over-hunted.

✓ **Geological events.** Natural occurrences such as earthquakes, extreme floods, and mudslides wipe out species. Widespread extinction occurred 65 million years ago, for example. Some scientists believe a huge **meteor** (falling matter from space) crashed into the Earth. This event, combined with other natural disasters like volcanic eruptions, may have helped kill the dinosaurs.

✓ **Habitat destruction.** People destroy ecosystems through logging, mining, pollution, and **deforestation**. In Borneo, people have cleared forests to make way for palm oil plantations. They have destroyed the endangered orangutan's habitat.

✓ **Invasive species.** Tree snakes invaded the island of Guam after World War II. How? They hid on ships from their native South Pacific. In a new habitat, tree snakes preyed on Guam's reptiles. They devoured the island's birds, and several species became extinct. (The invaders caused massive power outages, too. They slithered up power poles and across electrical lines.)

Higher temperatures have melted ice platforms polar bears use to hunt. Polar bear populations are lower as a result.

Protecting endangered species

Laws protect endangered species. You've learned bald eagles soared off the endangered species list in 2007. After the United States government banned DDT in the 1970s, eagles' eggs gradually grew less fragile. The eagle population slowly increased. In the UK during the 1960s, the sparrow hawk population declined. Why? The predators devoured prey that had been contaminated with DDT and other pesticides. Sparrow hawks produced eggs with thin shells. Fortunately, after the government banned DDT in the 1980s, sparrow hawk populations grew again.

Organizations comprised of concerned people work to protect and preserve endangered species and their habitats. In 2004, the United Kingdom's People's Trust for Endangered Species sounded an alarm about the Scottish wildcat.

Scottish wildcats

At one time, wildcats prowled much of Britain. The population diminished through habitat destruction. Feral cats, once raised as pets but released in the wild, pose another threat. They mate with wildcats and create **hybrids**. Hybrids are a mix between wildcat and feral cat. Today, fewer than 400 purebred wildcats remain. They live only in the Scottish Highlands.

Purebred Scottish wildcats hover on the brink of extinction.

Ferocious predators resemble pets

Scottish wildcats resemble tabby cats, one of the world's most popular pets. Both have striped bodies and bushy, ringed tails with black tips. Yet, the tabby is **domesticated**. It's accustomed to sharing a life with people. Not the wildcat. It's a fierce predator. Some scientists believe the cat, even raised in captivity, is completely untamable.

Tabby cats closely resemble the wildcat.

Research an endangered animal

- Select one or more of the following endangered animals: bobcat, killer whale, manatee, panda bear, leatherback sea turtle, macaw, gorilla, kiwi bird.

- Next, use print and online sources to find out about the animal and why it's endangered.

- Then, copy and complete the chart to share your findings.

Animal	Where It Lives	Why It's Endangered	How People Are Helping

Did you know?

Over 1,900 years ago, Ancient Romans first introduced domesticated cats to Britain.

The Roman army kept cats as good luck charms. When the cats arrived in Britain, they mated with wildcats. Later, when the Roman army departed, they left their cats behind. People took the strays into their homes as pets.

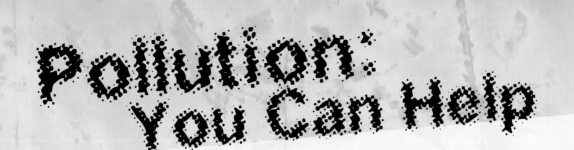

Pollution: You Can Help

Ecosystems are interconnected. When changes occur in one area, the entire system responds. Pollution disrupts and damages ecosystems.

This satellite image shows the lights of Europe at night. Light pollution impacts many plants and animals by changing their environment. These effects are felt throughout the ecosystem—from night-blooming flowers, plankton, and moths, to migratory birds, frogs, and salamanders.

Types of Pollution

- **Air pollution.** Auto exhaust, cigarette smoke, and industrial emissions (substances released from places like factories) pollute our air. Burning fuels release carbon dioxide gas, which contributes to global warming.

- **Light pollution.** Streetlights and flashing neon signs cast an artificial glow. Light pollution doesn't just obstruct your view of stars. It confuses wildlife, especially migratory birds. They depend on stars to find their way.

- **Land pollution.** People destroy ecosystems through deforestation, logging, and mining. They dump trash, everything from paper to rusty bikes, in landfills.

- **Water pollution.** A person tosses a plastic bottle in a lake. A factory dumps chemicals in a river. A tanker spills oil in the ocean. Human activities pollute water. They destroy aquatic food chains and harm drinking water.

CREATE AN OUTDOOR COMPOST

How can you help? Don't add food scraps and yard wastes to landfills. Send them back into the soil by **composting** waste! Ask for an adult to help.

- Your area may have specific composting regulations. Check first.
- You'll need gardening gloves, a compost bin, newspapers, dry leaves, food scraps, yard waste, water, a thermometer, and a pitchfork.
- Protect your hands with the gloves. Add "brown" items to the bin. These sources of carbon include newspapers and dry leaves.
- Add a layer of "green" items. These sources of nitrogen include grass clippings, apple cores, and eggshells.
- Keep layering browns and greens.
- Moisture and air speed the process. Add water, but don't soak the pile.
- The pile will heat up. After a few days, check it with the thermometer. Is the temperature about 60–70 °C (140–160 °F)?
- Don't add meat or fish to the compost. They're dangerous, and they'll smell terrible. They'll also attract pests.
- With an adult's help, use the pitchfork daily to turn the pile. In time, crumbly dark material should develop.
- Thoroughly wash your hands afterwards.

You've learned a balanced ecosystem has defined boundaries. It requires the Sun's energy. It's made up of living organisms, such as plants and animals, and dead ones, such as decaying animals. Nonliving things, including water and rocks, are also part of an ecosystem.

Visit a natural area. Make certain you have permission, since you might not be able to dig in certain areas. Then select an ecosystem to explore. For example, you might choose a schoolyard, a wooded lot, or the land near a lake or stream.

You'll need:

- Gardening gloves
- Copy of the chart on page 43
- Pen
- Small gardening shovel
- Magnifying glass

Explore

- Select one target area to investigate. You might pick a sunny clearing or a shady corner.

- Study your surroundings. What living things do you observe? What nonliving things are present?

Copy and complete the chart

- Note the living and nonliving items on the chart.

- Look for a water source. If there is one, describe it on the chart.

- Note the amount of sunlight. Record it on the chart.

- Wear gardening gloves for protection. Use caution when touching items in the ecosystem. Plants can cause **allergic reactions**. They might contain thorns.

- With the shovel, dig up a soil sample.

- With the magnifying glass, examine the soil. Describe the sample on the chart.

Clean up

- Carefully return the soil sample to its original position. Pat it in place with the shovel.

- Don't disrupt the ecosystem. Leave everything as you found it.

Sample completed chart

Location	Water Source	Level of Sunlight	Living Things	Nonliving Things	Soil Description
Field next to school	Small pond borders field	Very bright	Rabbits, squirrels, butterflies, bees, flies	Rocks, gravel, sunlight, soil	Moist, rich earth with worms inside

Quiz

Check what you learned by answering these questions.

1 Ecology is the study of relationships between what?
a. parasites and hosts
b. biomes and ecosystems
c. food chains and energy pyramids
d. living things and their environment

2 An ecosystem is a group of interdependent living and nonliving things that all live where?
a. in the same environment
b. in the wilderness
c. in parasitic relationships
d. in cities and suburbs

3 The struggle for survival between species for identical resources is what?
a. parasitism
b. succession
c. competition
d. ecosystem

4 Which of the following is an example of air pollution?
a. glaring city lights
b. oil spills
c. industrial emissions
d. deforestation

5 Which of these is an example of an act of nature that impacts an ecosystem?
a. a dust storm that destroys a wheat field
b. a farmer who clears trees so cattle can graze
c. a factory that dumps chemicals in a lake
d. a fire that campers accidentally start on a mountain

Answers on page 47.

Glossary

aggressive likely to attack or confront

allergic reaction physical reaction to a substance

aquatic found in or depending on water

biomagnification process in which a dangerous substance, such as a pesticide, increases at each level of the food chain

biomass renewable organic material, such as wood

burrow hole or tunnel dug by an animal, often as a home

carbohydrate natural compound which is in living things and many foods. Sugar is a kind of carbohydrate.

carnivore meat-eating animal

cell smallest functioning unit of an organism

chlorophyll green chemical in plants

chloroplast plant organelle in which photosynthesis takes place

community all the living things that live and interact in a natural area

competition struggle for survival between species for the same resources

composting process of decaying organic matter so it can be used as fertilizer

consumer animal that feeds on producers

decomposer fungi, bacteria, and insects that eat waste and break down nutrients from the dead

deforestation process of clearing or cutting down an area of trees or forest

domesticated adapted to life with people

ecologist scientist who studies organisms and how they relate to each other and their environment

ecology study of relationships between living things and their environment.

ecosystem a group of living and nonliving things that live in the same environment and rely on one another for survival

electronics devices that use electricity

environment natural surroundings

food chain line of organisms that depend on one another for survival. Each organism provides food for the next organism in the chain.

forage search for food

fungi group of plant-like organisms that produce spores, such as mushrooms

global warming slow increase in the temperature of the earth's atmosphere, due in part to pollution

herbivore plant-eating animal

hybrid animal that is made when animals from two separate species mate

invasive species plant or animal that is not native to a particular area. They become problems because they out-compete native species.

lichen simple plant formed from algae and fungus

meteor object from space that enters Earth's atmosphere

microorganism tiny organism

mining digging in the earth to find things such as gold or minerals

mutualism kind of symbiosis in which both creatures gain something

niche organism's role in an ecosystem

nocturnal active at night

omnivore animal that eats both plants and animals

parasitism symbiotic relationship in which one species benefits and the other does not

pesticide chemical that kills insects

photosynthesis process in which green plants use energy from the Sun to make their own food

pigment substance that makes color

pore tiny opening in the skin or surface of an organism

producer basic level of all food chains. Plants are producers.

regurgitate bring swallowed food up again.

respire process plants go through to use energy from food. The plants use oxygen to break down sugar.

stomata tiny pores in the outer layers of plants that take in air and allow water to pass

symbiosis relationship between two species which may be beneficial for only one or both species

terrestrial found on or related to land

Find Out More

Books

Freedman, Jeri. ***Climate Change: Human Effects on the Nitrogen Cycle***. Buffalo, NY: Rosen, 2007.

Housel, Debra J. ***Ecosystems***. Mankato, MN: Compass Point, 2009.

Morgan, Sally. ***Protecting Threatened Species***. Chicago: Heinemann, 2009.

Royston, Angela. ***Energy of the Future***. Chicago: Heinemann, 2008.

Websites

http://kids.nceas.ucsb.edu/ecology/ecoindex.html
Great site on ecology with a lot of good links, too.

http://www.wwfus.org/
The World Wildlife Fund exists to protect endangered species and protect their habitats.

http://www.envirolink.org/
This website provides up-to-date news and information on the environment.

Quiz answers

1. d, **2**. a, **3**. c, **4**. c, **5**. a.

Index